D1545012

CRACOW
Wawel – Old City – Kazimierz

100 photographs
by JANUSZ PODLECKI

Text
by GRAŻYNA ROTTER

CRACOW

WAWEL – OLD CITY – KAZIMIERZ

100 photographs
by JANUSZ PODLECKI

Text
by GRAŻYNA ROTTER

PUBLISHED BY WYDAWNICTWO „KARPATY" — ANDRZEJ ŁĄCZYŃSKI & RHEMA
CRACOW 1995

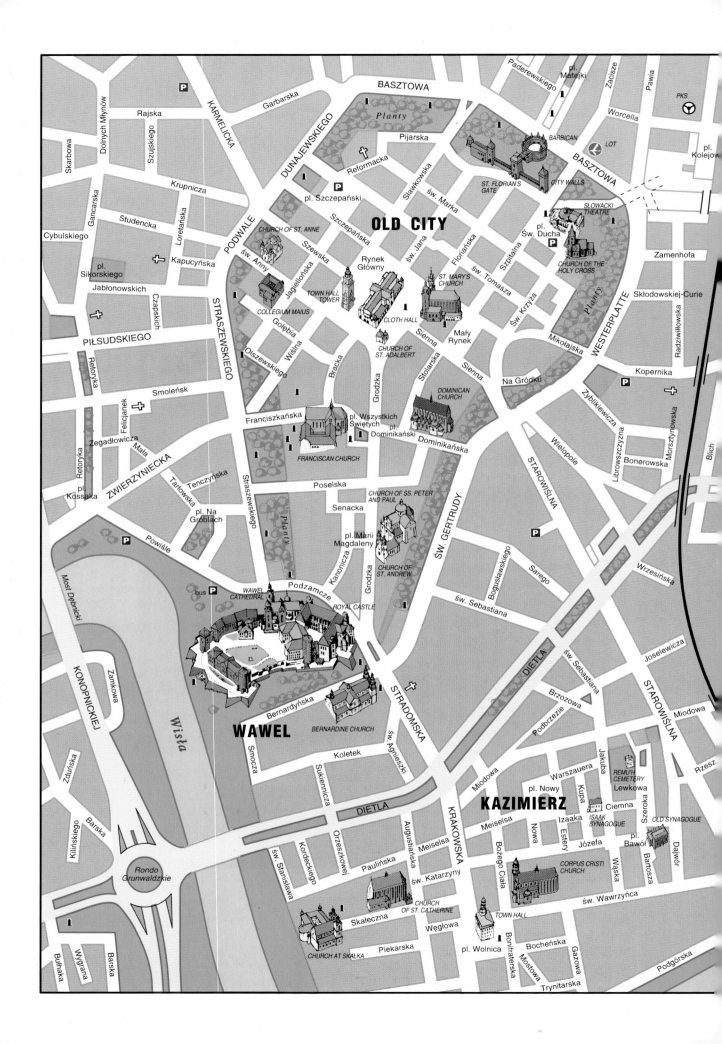

CRACOW

with its 750 thousand inhabitants, is among the biggest Polish cities. Yet its renown, which has reached beyond Poland and Europe, is based neither on its size nor on its economic significance. The city on the Vistula, the cradle and centre of Polish statehood, has been known predominantly as the nucleus of Polish national culture, as a city of thousands of unique old buildings which have survived numerous wars unscathed, and as a dynamic centre of science, its tradition going back six centuries.

In the early Middle Ages Cracow was the main seat of the Slav tribe of the Vistulanians, and it was probably then, in the 7th century, that the two mounds, of Krak and Wanda, were erected. In the 10th century Prince Mieszko I annexed Cracow and the land of the Vistulanians to the Polish State. In 1000 a bishopric was established in Cracow and the construction od the first cathedral was begun. Ca 1038 Prince Casimir the Restorer made Cracow his capital, and first stone buildings were built on Wawel Hill. In 1138 Boleslaus III Wrymouth chose the town as the seat of the Senior Prince when Poland was split into several provinces.

After ravages by the Tartars in 1241, Prince Boleslaus the Chaste granted a charter to Cracow in 1257 and drew the city plan which has survived unchanged, with a regular grid of streets and a central square market place. From the 13th to the 15th centuries the stone and brick City Walls were built, encompassing the city and joining it with Wawel Castle.

In the reign of King Casimir the Great (1333–1370) the city and Wawel were thoroughly rebuilt in the Gothic style. The King settled the borough of Kazimierz to the south of Cracow and founded Cracow Academy, the predecessor of the oldest Polish university, the Jagellonian University.

The city flourished in the 16th century under the last kings of the Jagellon dynasty, when a number of fine Renaissance buildings were erected. The period of the Vasa dynasty, particularly the reign of King Sigismund III Vasa, was marked by the lavish proliferation of the Baroque.

In 1609 Sigismund III Vasa moved the royal seat to Warsaw, yet Cracow remained the place of the coronation of the Polish kings and of their burial; it retained the title of the royal capital city. In the mid-17th century Cracow was sacked by Swedish troops, which looted it again in the early 18th century. The year 1734 saw the last coronation in Wawel Cathedral, of Augustus III of the Saxon dynasty.

After the First Partition of Poland in 1772 Cracow found itself near the country's southern border. After the Second Partition, in 1794, a national insurrection started in Cracow, and its leader, Tadeusz Kościuszko, took an oath to the nation in the Market Square. After the suppression of the Insurrection and the Third Partition the city was taken over by Austria. In 1809 it was joined with the Grand Duchy of Warsaw. After Napoleon's defeat, the Congress of Vienna proclaimed Cracow a Free City (1815). In that period of limited autonomy the remains of the national heroes, Tadeusz Kościuszko and Prince Józef Poniatowski, were buried at Wawel, and a mound in honour of the Insurrection leader was erected at St. Bronisława's Hill. After Cracow's autonomy was abolished in 1846, the Austrians turned Wawel Castle into military barracks again, encircled Wawel Hill with fortifications and built a line of defences around the city.

In 1918, after over a century of foreign rule, Cracow became independent again. The years of World War II were marked by the extinction of the Jews in Kazimierz and the rule of Governor General Hans Frank, who resided at Wawel Castle. On 18th January 1945 the city was liberated by Soviet troops. In the post-war period it expanded rapidly and developed into a large industrial centre, with large steel works; the resulting environmental degradation has become one of the most difficult problems for the city to solve.

In 1978 the UNESCO Organization listed Cracow as a monument of world cultural heritage.

WAWEL

The high limestone Wawel Hill, which rises in the centre of the city, holds a treasure of historical monuments which are a symbol of Poland's history and culture.

The first traces of human residence at Wawel go back 50 thousand years. Until the 17th century it was the seat of the Polish kings. The Royal Castle, of predominantly Renaissance character, was built by Italian architects, commissioned by King Sigismund the Old, in the years 1502–1536. Some of the rooms are furnished in the Renaissance style, some in the Baroque style. The north-eastern part of the Castle contains the Treasury and the Armoury, and in the western part a collection of Eastern art is exhibited.

The Gothic Cathedral is another fine building on Wawel Hill. It is surrounded by a ring of chapels, with the pearl of Renaissance art, the Sigismund Chapel. Almost all Polish kings, beginning with Ladislaus the Short (d. 1333), were crowned in the Cathedral. It was also the place of royal funerals and burials, and later received the remains of national heroes and great poets.

The vestiges of the oldest constructions on Wawel Hill can be seen at the exhibition "The Lost Wawel". The Cathedral Museum presents mainly items from the Cathedral Treasury.

In the Wawel fortifications the most impressive are the Senators' Tower, the Sandomierz Tower and the Thieves' Tower, as well as the brick walls which run along the hill perimeter; they were built, together with bastions and gates, by the Austrians in the 19th century.

At the western part of the Hill there is an entrance which leads down to the Dragon's Cave, which features in the ancient legend about the dragon once residing at the foot of Wawel.

← 1. View of the Vistula, Wawel and Skałka

2. Wawel Hill seen from the Vistula

3. Night view of Wawel

← 4. Wawel seen from the Vistula

5. View of Wawel Cathedral from Straszewskiego Street

6. Wawel Hill with a bend of the Vistula

9. A section of the Castle Walls with a turret →

7. The Sandomierz Tower

8. The Senators' Tower

10. The Castle Walls seen from Podzamcze Street

12. A part of the Royal Castle seen from Stradom Street –

13. A section of the arcaded Court of the Royal Castle –

11. Wawel Hill and the Vistula

14. The Senators' Room in the Royal Castle

15. An arras tapestry from the lanscape-and-fauna series, the collection of King Sigismund Augustus

16. The Envoys' Room in the Royal Castle

17. The Rotunda of S.S. Felix and Adauctus (10th c.), a part of "The Lost Wawel" exhibition

19. Wawel Cathedral →

18. Wawel Cathedral and the Senators' Tower (right); in the foreground the outline of the foundations of Gothic churches

20. The Sigismund Tower of Wawel Cathedral

21. The Sigismund Bell in Wawel Cathedral

23. The nave of Wawel Cathedral ‒

22. A section of Wawel Cathedral with the golden dome of the Renaissance Sigismund Chapel

24. The tomb of Queen Jadwiga in Wawel Cathedral

25. The silver coffin with St. Stanislaus' relics in Wawel Cathedral

26. The tomb of King Casimir the Great in Wawel Cathedral

27. The royal insignia in the Cathedral Treasury

28. The reliquary of St. Stanislaus' head in the Cathedral Treasury

THE OLD CITY

holds most of the finest monuments and museums in Cracow.

The oldest part of Cracow is outlined by the Planty — a four-kilometer-long green belt which in the 19th century replaced the demolished medieval city walls and the moat which once encircled the city. Some elements of those fortifications have survived, namely the unique 15th-century Barbican and a section of the walls with four towers and St. Florian's Gate.

The Market Square is particulary remarkable; this largest (200 m x 200 m) and most beautiful square in Cracow for seven centuries, witnessed a number of historic events, including the homage paid to King Sigsmund the Old by Duke Albert of Prussia and the oath sworn by Kościuszko. Among the most important buildings are the Gothic St. Mary's Church, with the High Altar carved by Wit Stwosz (Veit Stoss), the Cloth Hall, a busy trading centre which dates from the reign of Casimir the Great and was later rebuilt in the Renaissance style, the 13th-century Town Hall Tower, as well as many mainly Renaissance and Baroque houses and palaces. Other famous historic buildings in the Old Town are the 15th-century Collegium Maius, the oldest seat of the Jagellonian University, and St. Anne's Church, the finest baroque church in Cracow.

Among the many museums in the Old Town the most recommended are: the Czartoryski Museum, with its fine collections of paintings, crafts, items which once belonged to the monarchs, and ancient art; the Gallery of Polish Painting and Sculpture in the Cloth Hall, with a rich collection of Polish, mainly 19th-century painting; the Historical Museum of the City of Cracow, whose exhibits tell the story of the city and its culture; the Museum of the Jagellonian University in the Collegium Maius, with an unique collection which presents the history of the University.

← 29. A game of chess at the foot of Wawel Hill

30. The Grunwald Monument in Matejko Square and the Barbican, in the background the towers of St. Florian's Gate and St. Mary's Church

31. A section of the Planty, with the
Barbican and the towers in the
City Walls, in the background
St. Mary's Church (right)

33. The Barbican seen from
St. Florian's Gate →

32. St. Florian's Gate seen from the
Planty

34. An evening at the Planty

35. A section of the Planty

36. The Haberdashers' Tower seen from the Planty

37. St. Florian's Gate and a section of the medieval City Walls

38. The Joiners' Tower and the old City Arsenal seen from the Planty

40. A section of Floriańska Street with the Jan Matejko House —

39. A section of the buildings of the Czartoryski Museum in Pijarska Street

41. The Gothic Church of the Holy Cross

42. The Juliusz Słowacki Theatre

3. The late-Gothic vault in the Holy Cross Church supported by a single pillar

44. St. John's Church

45. View of St. Mary's Church from Starowiślna Street

46. A street musican

48. View of St. Mary's Church from Floriańska Street →

47. The western side of the Little Market Square

49. St. Mary's Church and the Market Square

50. A section of the nave at St. Mary's Church

51. The medieval High Altar by Wit Stwosz at St. Mary's

52. Tne central section of the medieval altar by Wit Stwosz

53. The Renaissance ciborium (for the Eucharist) at St. Mary's

54. The fountain in St. Mary's Square

56. View from St. Mary's Square toward the Cloth Hall and the Town Hall Tower →

55. The 15th-century crucifix at St. Mary's, carved by Wit Stwosz

58. View of the Cloth Hall
from Szewska Street

57. St. Mary's Church, the Cloth Hall and the Town Hall Tower

60. The Cloth Hall

← 59. The Cloth Hall cloisters from Szewska Street

61. A section of the Cloth Hall

62. A section of the Market Square with St. Mary's Church and the Adam Mickiewicz Monument

63. The Adam Mickiewicz Monument

64. The Cloth Hall at night

65. Night view of the Market Square with St. Adalbert's Church

67. A section of the Market Square with St. Adalbert's Church and St. Mary's Church

← 66. The Town Hall Tower

68. Sculptures, St. Adalbert's Church

69. St. Adalbert's Church

70. A room in the famous Wierzynek Restaurant

71. A horse-drawn omnibus in the Market Square

72. Antiques sale in front of the Cloth Hall

3. The Lajkonik in the Market Square

74. A folk ensemble performs in the Market Square

75. Cracovian women in folk costumes

76. A Cracovian male in a folk costume

77. A traditional Corpus Christi procession

78–81. The Juvenalia — the annual revels of Cracow students

2. A procession od the Marksmen's Brotherhood in the Market Square

3. The Markemen's King with the silver cock, the symbol of the Brotherhood

84. The Collegium Maius of the Jagellonian University

86. The collection of astronomical instruments in the Jagellonian University Museum, Collegium Maius →

85. A section of the Collegium Maius Court

87. The Green Room in the Collegium Maius

89. The Romanesque St. Andrew's Church →

88. The Libraria (the former library) in the Collegium Maius

KAZIMIERZ

The old borough of Kazimierz, now within the city centre, was founded in 1335 by King Casimir the Great, who intended it to be a rival to Cracow where burghers were mainly of German descent. Its centre was a vast market place, not much smaller than the Cracow one, and the borough was encircled by walls, whose remains can be still seen. In the late 15th century Jews were moved from Cracow to Kazimierz; they lived there for centuries, until World War II, enjoying autonomy. Therefore, apart from monuments of Polish history and culture, Kazimierz is particularly rich in the evidence of a specific and unique Jewish material and spiritual culture.

Polish history and tradition is best symbolized in the Church Na Skałce (the present 18th-century church was built on the site of the old Romanesque one). According to legend, Stanislaus, Bishop of Cracow, was killed there. The Polish kings used to make a pilgrimage to that church before their coronation. The crypt now contains the tombs of distinguished Poles. Other remarkable churches are the large three-ailed basilica of the Augustinian Canons, the purest example of Gothic architecture in Cracow, and the 14th-century Corpus Christi Church. In Wolnica Square, which is what has remained of the original vast market place, stands the 15th-century Town Hall, much altered in later periods. It houses the Ethnographic Museum.

Jewish history and culture is represented by the Old Synagogue, the oldest synagogue in Poland, originally Gothic but later rebuilt in the Renaissance style. Now it houses the Judaic Museum. Another fine complex consists of the 16th-century Remu'h Synagogue and the adjacent cemetery; this smallest of the synagogues in Kazimierz is the only one where the Orthodox Jews worship nowadays.

90. The Paulite Church at Skałka: the crypt with the tombs of distinguished Poles

91. St. Catherine's Church from Skałeczna Street, in the background the tower of Corpus Christi Church

92. The former Town Hall in Kazimierz, now the Ethnographic Musem

94. The interior of the Old Synagogue, now a museum

← 93. View from Wolnica Square towards the Gothic Corpus Christi Church

95. The Old Synagogue is the oldest synagogue in Poland

96. A section of the Jewish Remu'h Cemetery, one of the oldest in Europe

97. Józefa (Joseph) Street near the High Synagogue

8. Ariel Cafe

99. An alley in Kazimierz

00. Mykwa (Jewish ritual bath) at the corner of Miodowa and Dajwór Streets

Published in cooperation with
RHEMA PUBLISHERS
31-033 Kraków, ul. Westerplatte 8, Tel./Fax (0-12) 22-59-43, Centertel (0-90) 33-03-36

Graphic design:
JULIAN PRZEMYSKI

Plan:
MARIUSZ SZELEREWICZ

Photographs:

JANUSZ PODLECKI

Translated into English by
JADWIGA PIĄTKOWSKA

ISBN 83-85204-18-0

PUBLISHED BY WYDAWNICTWO „KARPATY" — ANDRZEJ ŁĄCZYŃSKI
30-074 Kraków, ul. Kazimierza Wielkiego 21, Tel./Fax (0-4812) 33-62-13